The OPTIMIST

MUSTAFA MUN

notionpress.com

INDIA • SINGAPORE • MALAYSIA

Notion Press

No.8, 3rd Cross Street
CIT Colony, Mylapore
Chennai, Tamil Nadu – 600004

First Published by Notion Press 2020
Copyright © Mustafa Mun 2020
All Rights Reserved.

ISBN 978-1-63606-690-5

CONTENTS

PREFACE

The following pages are a compilation of my experience and interpretation of the transitions induced by COVID – 19. Like everyone else, I was shocked by the sudden changes in the world. For a while, it felt like everything was destroyed. But my academic background and determination for progress allowed me to fight and survive. And now I want you to benefit from my diary of COVID – 19 recovery. I saw a silver lining when the cloud of COVID – 19 enveloped the world, and after reading the book you will be able to find the light of opportunities as well.

I did my higher education in England, completed bachelors in management and obtained a doctorate in clinical psychology. At present, I am practising as well as managing the family business, which is into manufacturing.

My acute sense of value of human feelings and emotions motivated me to work on this subject. Additionally, my academic and business experiences allowed me to frame the subject well. You can heal an injury only when you have studied it thoroughly and understood it. When the spread of COVID – 19 was arousing fear in every household I was busy studying its effect on business and your lifestyle.

COVID – 19 has damaged multitudes of industries and aspects of the world. So, I felt the need to highlight ways of recovering from these injuries. While researching the topic I found that it is more convenient to understand a subject in stages. First, I studied the scenario before COVID – 19. Then I focused on Life after COVID – 19. Next, I analysed both the periods and understood the changes brought by COVID – 19 in a detailed manner.

Once I was well versed with the problem, I started to find informed solutions. Fortunately, I was able to apply my solutions practically to myself and my business. Some solutions worked well while some brought disappointments. I captured the solutions with the best results. Therefore, I can present before you, tried and tested methods to deal with the ill-effects of COVID – 19.

Since I discovered the importance of learning in stages, I employed a similar approach to structure this book. You will be able to understand your situation gradually and then find the solution in the conclusion.

INTRODUCTION

All of us know about COVID – 19 and the impact of this novel Coronavirus on the health of people across the world. But have you thought how this pandemic impacted the world's economy?

COVID – 19 started as a disease, but slowly it stretched its wings to adversely affect the social, political, and economic aspects of the world. In the economic sphere, stock markets around the world have seen a rapid fall ranging from 5-20%. Hiring rates have been impacted and most countries reported their real growth rates in the negative.

The pandemic has altered mental health, family, money, business and, in short, the value of everything. This crisis has successfully drawn a bold line between the time before COVID – 19 and after COVID – 19. It was like an external force interfered with the functioning of this world and altered almost everything in existence.

Even a few weeks before the outbreak of COVID – 19, the world had no idea of the looming transformations. The universe is changing every second, but with the introduction of the novel Coronavirus, everything changed simultaneously and significantly. There was no warning and no preparation.

All of a sudden, terms like quarantine, lockdown, and social distancing were echoing throughout the world. Schools were closing, and migrants were returning to their homes. Everyone wanted a safe and secure place to live. Suddenly the warm gestures of handshakes and hugs transformed into horrifying customs. People started to maintain distance from each other and were frightened by even the mildest sneeze of others.

COVID – 19 changed everything. Try to remember the last time you shook hands with a stranger without using a sanitizer. I am sure if you are a careful and responsible person, then the answer is, before the widespread COVID – 19.

The methods of social interaction are the first and most evident change brought about by COVID – 19. Earlier, or in the days before COVID – 19, you used to greet formally through a handshake and informally probably through a hug. But after COVID – 19, social distancing has become the new mantra of social interaction. A verbal greet suffices for meetings now.

The ubiquitous use of the term 'new normal' is evidence that the world is moving towards a new age following new norms and new regulations.

The effects of COVID – 19 are grave and global. One way or the other COVID – 19 tries to attack all of us. Either through our health (mental and physical) or our financial books it penetrates our life. Even if a person is physically healthy, the fear of this pandemic could severely damage his mental health.

Everyone is trying to adjust to the new normal. The whole world is under threat, and we all have to get through these difficult times together.

Remember the evening when you were sitting beside your window glancing at the astonishing sunset and wondering what wonders the world will see with the new day. Before all this, you might have been worrying about your studies, work, or relationship issues unaware of the fact that all your tensions are going to become insignificant in comparison to COVID – 19. With the spread of this pandemic, our priorities changed, perceptions transformed, powers shifted, and participation took on a new hue.

When COVID – 19 was changing the world, a part of each one's life also got replaced. The perception of the fundamental unit of an economy, money, was broken. The functioning of the drivers of the economy, businesses also changed. We all wished to go back to the old normal. But the effect is so grave that no one could bring back the pre-COVID – 19 days for now.

The change in the functioning of businesses may have shocked you, but you have to stand firm and deal with these changes. You have to analyze the difference and figure out how to develop your business according to the new norms. The effects of COVID – 19 on the economy require new strategies and new methods for successfully running businesses. You have to formulate effective strategies to optimize your business and achieve novel goals after the pandemic.

Your aim is to support your business. The effects of this pandemic are too dreadful to be repaired overnight. For reaching the stage of effective strategies, first you have to study the effects of COVID 19 on the economic health of the world. Then you shall analyse the changes brought by this pandemic in your business that works under the umbrella of global economy. Only after careful research, will you be able to decide what is best for you and your business.

The lockdown forced everyone to remain within the four walls of their house, but nothing could stop the increasing speed of change. People were worrying. They were panicking. They were confused. They are still confused. A difference as big as COVID – 19 tends to leave a significant impact on everyone. It requires strength and time to deal with the changes. You cannot expect to wake up one morning and adjust to the new normal. You have to go slowly, and then you will learn to survive in life after COVID – 19.

You cannot expect the old times, norms, and regulations to come back after witnessing a global crisis such as COVID – 19. Looking back is not an option. Looking forward is your path to survive and succeed today. You have to be strong and sound, mentally and physically. COVID – 19 has changed a lot around you, and this book is here to help you in dealing with the changes.

Don't worry if the sudden changes have surprised you. Don't panic if you don't know how to cope up with the change. Don't get stressed thinking that you won't be able to keep up in the race of the ever-changing world. Just take a deep breath and keep reading. Your surroundings might have changed, but you haven't. Your views might have changed, but your will hasn't. The methods might have changed, but your aims haven't. All you need to do is be equipped with information, new techniques, and determination.

Digitization was bringing changes in the world, but COVID – 19 introduced to us the new limits of technologies. Organizations were not aware of their technological powers until they were forced to use them due to the effects of COVID – 19. Work from home, lockdown, and digital offices have changed the course of businesses.

This book is my attempt to help you in understanding the effects of COVID – 19 efficiently and formulating effective and gainful strategies for development. You will find a few essential economic concepts that affect your life regularly, such as money and business. You will be able to unleash the facts regarding the changes brought by COVID – 19 and move closer to success in the new world after COVID – 19. Complex concepts have been simplified for you and your upcoming success.

Don't worry. You do not need any technical knowledge to understand the chapters. The following pages are written for you to understand the effect of COVID – 19 easily. The main aim is to help you to grab the changes like a ladder of opportunities and support you to climb your way towards success and stability.

The spread of COVID – 19 has given birth to a lot of questions. The first one being: What about my health? Then gradually raising the question about my job? My business? And my money? But my friend, your questions are going to be answered soon. Your determination is going to build soon.

Information and understanding are the foundation for successful strategies. When you gain information about a situation and understand it well, you tend to plan your actions ingeniously. Undoubtedly, it is difficult to rise after the blow dealt by COVID – 19, but it is not impossible. It is time for you to adjust to the changes, plans, and progress.

Your business, life, perception of money might have witnessed a shift due to this pandemic. But it is your responsibility to optimize these shifts and use it as an opportunity to strengthen your business and life. Allow this book to assist you in succeeding in life after COVID – 19. Maintaining your physical health, mental health, and business health is the mantra for the period known as 'After COVID – 19.' First, learn about the differences, then learn how to deal with them and then progress and prosper.

LIFE BEFORE COVID – 19

Value of Money

In economic terms, the value of money means the number of goods and services that money could purchase. But for the human mind, the value of money is much more. For you and everybody around you, money is a more precious term than just a means. The value of money kept changing even before the dreadful spread of COVID – 19. But no shift was as grave as the effect of COVID – 19. Common commodities like onion and tomato were selling double their usual price as the supply chain got disrupted due to the pandemic.

Perception of Money

Exchange of commodities and services means a deal between a seller and a buyer, where the seller hands the goods or provides the service to the buyer, and the buyer pays the price for the goods or services in the form of money. Thus, money is the means. But through all these years of industrial development, you have noticed that the perception of money has also altered. From just a means, it has become the end goal of life. You have seen people struggle in daily life to procure money. We sweated, We fought, We cried, and We tried, all intending to earn money.

The intriguing fact is that the story did not end with the possession of money. The real value of money came to light after you procured a certain amount of money. While some people were focused on the question 'how to sustain and multiply my earnings', others were finding the answer to 'how to tell society that I have money'.

The first group revolved around investments and strategies. In comparison, the latter was focused on splurging on luxuries. Earning money through an exchange was just the beginning. We wanted to increase the value of the money we possessed. We wanted to buy goods worth the value of the money we had. You saw some people investing money in bonds and securities while others were busy buying jewellery to wear at evening parties. Some dedicated their whole life to earn money and forgot to value their life over money, while some used money just as a means to survive in society. Either way, we attributed to money more than its real value. All of us designed our life to revolve around money. First, we worked hard to earn money, and then we exhausted ourselves under the strain of using it.

Measuring the Value of Money Before COVID – 19

Money is not a stagnant concept. Money is always flowing. The value of money is a subjective variable. It is upon the person holding the money to decide whether to invest or to spend, whether to add or subtract. Before the outbreak of COVID – 19, you must have noticed that the majority of the population failed to perceive the real value of money and somewhere the actual value of life. When they thought that earning money is the aim of life, they began to measure the value of life in terms of money.

According to economists, the value of commodities and services is measured in terms of money, and the value of money is measured in terms of the goods and services it can buy.

However, according to philosophers, the value of money is a subjective concept. Some may value money more than human life, paid assassins, for example. At the same time, some may value money just as a mere means of exchange, which comes and goes along with time. Many factors influence your interpretation of the importance of money. The functioning of society is the most significant influencer on the value of money. Social affairs and interaction dominate your thoughts and tend to influence your interpretations. Even the tiniest event in your life holds the power to change your point of view. For example, COVID – 19 has successfully changed everyone's understanding of almost everything in the world. Before the pandemic you used to prioritise money over your health, but now you know that health is wealth.

However, different people have different opinions and interpretations. Different events affect people differently. For example, after COVID – 19 some people panicked after the lockdown was announced and stocked their homes with many unnecessary products. But most of the people were patient and saved their money for emergencies and invested only in useful things.

To Earn to Live or Live to Earn?

Undoubtedly, money is the means to buy the basic needs for survival such as food, shelter, and clothes. But for some people, the value of money goes beyond the purpose of survival. For some, money is not only a means to survive, but it is the ultimate goal of human life. In their words, 'you live to earn money.' The question was: Is it the correct interpretation? Or is the reality upside down? Do you live to earn money or earn money for a living?

These questions were going to be answered by the pandemic. We were tangled in these concerns, unaware that all our beliefs were going to change. No one knew that an epidemic would change their perception. Some were earning money for a living while others were living for earning money, oblivious to the changes that the spread of COVID – 19 would bring about in the value of money, in man's perception of money, and the interpretation of the importance of money.

You know better which group you belong to. You know very well how you valued money and what were your views regarding the complex concept of money. And you also feel that the pandemic has altered your perception. You know how to use your money and what your perception was before COVID – 19.

Use of Money

The use of money is an integral part of the value of money. You can easily deduce someone's perception of money by glancing at their bills. How a person spends or invests his money is indicative of the way he measures the value of money. Generally, the way you treat something is reflective of its value in your eyes, but in the case of money, it's how you use it that shows the value of money in your perception.

Change in circumstances also changed the way we see money. With only a few exceptions, it was COVID – 19 that woke up the majority of the world population.

For understanding the use of money better, let us divide the world population into three groups – low income, middle income, and high income. The priorities of these groups are different, their interpretation of money is different, and hence the use of money is different.

Low Income Group

The prime and only concern of people belonging to this group is the possession of necessities. They earn money to ensure food, shelter, and clothing. The less you have, the more you value it. For the low income group, possessing a large amount of money is not an easy task. Thus, they value the small amount of money they can earn. They restrict the use of money to buy necessities.

These people got most severely affected by the disruption in normal functioning. Most people ended up getting dependent on support programs.

Middle Income Group

The people who earn a little more than the value of necessities tend to spend on other goods and services as well. The middle income group used the money for numerous purposes other than food, shelter, and clothing, but the limit is not too far. Generally, disposable income was used for procuring essentials of better quality to ensure a higher standard of living. But some people intended to use the money to establish a higher social status.

People used to spend their money on luxuries and showcase goods and services. They used to feel that these luxuries helped them live a better life with a higher status in society. Little did they know that their beliefs were going to change.

The savings of middle income groups were severely impacted. A lot of them lost employment and their standard of living came down.

High Income Group

The higher the income, the excess money people have is spent on goods and services besides the basic needs for survival. The high income group used their money to procure high-quality necessities and a great number of luxuries, for money was the crown that allowed them to sit on the highest position in society. When people used to value money more than anything in the world, then the high income group became the top designated personalities in society. They invested their money to increase their returns and used their money smartly to display their wealth and power to the world.

These are the people who may be least affected by the disease. Their overall wealth decreased but they remained safe more or less.

The Prior Power of Money

Power is another variable in the value of money. We used to associate societal power with the value of money. The more money a person possesses, the higher is his power. The world hierarchy started to design itself according to the amount of money people possessed. It is not only the amount but also the goods and services they bought using that money. People in possession of the most expensive diamond in the world were referred to as powerful. The value of money had started to dominate the world and establish itself as the power and the aim of life.

We used money differently, but the majority aimed to survive with a higher standard of living. A higher standard refers to a lifestyle where people can easily access necessities of high quality.

The interpretation of the standard of living has also changed because of the pandemic. People who believed that higher standards were achieved through social validation were surprised by the flash of reality thrown by the pandemic.

Money Storage

Along with the perception, use and value of money, the method of possession was also different before COVID – 19. There are various ways you can store money such an in the form of bonds, investments, insurance, cash, etc. You can store money in the form of wealth. Wealth is the total worth of possessions belonging to a single person. Cash is the earliest and simplest form of storing money. It is portable and aids you in making easy payments for goods and services. With the development of the digital world and efforts like demonetization, the popularity of cash started to decline. We started to use digital payment methods and store money digitally. But still, some people believed in cash transactions. The popularity may have declined, but it was still widely used. However, the arrival of COVID – 19 changed it all. The storage of money determines the medium of business transactions. Thus, the pandemic infected your business transactions as well.

Working of Business

Before the term COVID – 19 was being used all over the world, the working of business was different. Business can be explained as a unit which deals with the exchange of products and services, considering the laws and welfare of the community. Every business is started with an objective, and to achieve a larger goal, various small time-based targets are set by each business.

It is the objective of every business to differentiate it from the others and guide you through the working. In simpler words, the functioning of a business is based on the objective set by the founders. For example, if you start a business to produce high-quality cosmetics, then during the lifetime of the business, all the departments included in the business will set their specific goals to ensure that they make the best quality of cosmetics available to the public. This is the primary goal of a business. For secondary goals, you can select profit maximization, community service, or any goal that you want to achieve to reach the primary objective.

You will observe variegated forms of business around you. The most basic categories of business are - small business and large business. The differences are not prominent because every business is a business and is concerned about the exchange of goods and services. Few quantitative variables differentiate a small business from a large business and also causes them to function differently. Qualitatively, all businesses are equal. COVID – 19 has had a serious impact on both categories.

Let us first understand how they worked before COVID – 19, and then we will compare it with the working after COVID – 19 and then decide how to help your business to develop in this time of global crisis.

Small Business

You can label business as small based on the number of employees, extent of operations and revenue. Small businesses tend to hire a smaller number of employees, limit their operations, and earn comparatively less than the larger businesses. You can recognize a small business from the beginning itself. The owner generally arranges the capital required to start a small business on his/her own. The general source includes the owner's savings, loans, or gifts from friends and relatives. Small businesses are usually owned by a sole proprietor or managed in partnerships. For the normal functioning of the business, investors may help with the financing.

Since the sources of financing are limited, the scope of growth is less in small businesses. The income is limited, and access to resources is restricted. Thus, small businesses function on a small scale. The prime advantage of small business is personal relations with the customers. Small businesses believe in close relations with stakeholders, including investors, existing customers, prospective customers, and the public as a whole. Though small businesses have limited access to resources, they are concerned about the welfare of society and often invest in the development of the community.

Generally, the functions of small business are carried out offline. Since small businesses value personal interactions, they avoid online and distant business activities. However, in the digital world, everyone is online in one way or the other. Maybe a business didn't have any social media account or website to collect orders online. Still, the younger members of the family promote the business through their social media handles. In a small business, grapevine communication is more popular than formal communication channels. Co-workers also have comfortable relations with one another, and the daily interaction and cosy setting of small businesses help them to increase their morale and productivity.

Regular social interactions and manual activities were the mantras for the functioning of small businesses, but COVID – 19 changed it all. In a small business, the hierarchical structure is also small. Since the budget is limited, only a few important departments function in small businesses, and thus the decision-making process is quick and effective. Delegation of responsibilities and rewarding authorities are easier as there are few numbers, which leads to a simple and small hierarchical structure. Thus, in small businesses, interpersonal relations are laudable and contribute towards the limited development of the business.

Large Business

A large business functions on a larger scale, with a higher number of employees and a greater scope for growth. The revenue is also greater than the small business. You will rarely find a sole proprietary or partnership business in the field of large businesses. The term only suggests that everything is larger in volume when it comes to large businesses, including revenue, personnel, resources, departments, and stakeholders. The large businesses are generally recognized as companies that are owned by shareholders who vote to elect the board of directors.

The capital of a large business is generally derived from shares, bonds, and other forms of security. In this system, equity shareholders exercise the right to vote regarding the top management of the company, while preferential shareholders just enjoy the profits of the company. A large business is less interested in establishing personal relations and keener in working professionally to increase the profits of the company. Unlike small businesses, there are legions of people involved in a large business. The number of stakeholders in large business exceeds the number of stakeholders in small business by a great amount. Thus, it is difficult for a large business to maintain personal relations with all of them. Larger business is more inclined to professional aspects than to the personal aspect.

A formal and complicated hierarchical structure is followed in a large business. Since the number of employees is high and the scale of operation is large, the functions are divided into several departments, with each department equipped with professionals and experts. The company has separate guidelines and objectives for each department as well. The management in a large business also differs from a small business. In large businesses, a board of directors is elected by the shareholders to formulate the top management. The decision-making process is lengthy and time-consuming.

As a result of the elaborate hierarchical structure, formal communication channels are more prevalent in a large business. Due to the large number of employees, it is difficult to establish a friendly relationship with one another. But formal interdepartmental coordination is ensured for effective results. If a subordinate wants to approach the top management, he has to pass numerous levels and use the proper channel of communication.

Large businesses ensure that he is taking advantage of all the opportunities available to them. And due to the easy access to resources, they can optimize various opportunities such as technology. Large businesses ensure that they make the best use of technology to produce the best result for the business. In large businesses, the employees may not be personally connected, but the resources ensure that they are virtually connected. However, many large businesses did not recognize their capabilities in the area of technology until the terrifying spread of the pandemic.

To understand better the difference between the working of business BEFORE and AFTER COVID – 19, we will study the functioning of a business divided into various departments that coordinate to build your business:

Various Departments in Business

1. Administration Department

As the name suggests, the administration of the whole business lies in the hand of the administration department, from decision making to imposition, every instruction is initiated from this department. The prime job of an administrative department is to supervise and ensure productive coordination among all the departments. For fulfilling this duty, the department always kept a close eye on the working of the business. You can look upon the administrative department as the head of all departments.

The communication from the top management initiates from here, and the communication for the lower level ends here.

It was simple and convenient for the administrative department to supervise the working of business before COVID – 19. But as you can see, COVID – 19 has affected everyone and everything. You will find an administrative department both in small and large businesses, though their size may differ.

2. Finance Department

The finance department deals with accounting and finance related functions. When you are running a business, it is essential to keep a formal record of all the business transactions. The finance department takes care of tax-related issues and payments and receipts of the business. Large businesses ensure that they have a prominent financial department equipped with professionals. Sometimes in a small business, you will find the owner playing the role of a whole financial department. Generally in small businesses, you will notice only one or two persons taking care of the accounting and finance functions. Finance departments require regular updates and efforts of experts working together to achieve the primary goals of the business.

Finance departments only allow the management to analyze the monetary progress of the business as well as decision on the budget. Before COVID – 19 resulted in the imposition of the lockdown, the finance department was working in coordination with all other departments, maintaining personal interactions, and often using manual labour.

3. Sales Department

It is simple; the sales department deals with the sales of the business. It arranges the sales, supervises records of the sales and performs various functions related to the sale of goods and services offered by a business. In some businesses, you will notice that they have merged the marketing and sales department to reduce the number of employees and maintain a small budget. Generally, in a large business, you will find separate sales and marketing departments. It may be cost-effective to merge the two departments, but to produce the best results, separate departments are always advisable. If each department has separate and clear goals, then the chances of effective functioning are more. The sales department is the closest to the customers, and thus social interactions are unavoidable for them.

4. Marketing Department

In the digital world, 'marketing' is a familiar term. One way or the other, you might have heard about marketing and also might be aware that it holds immense importance in the business world. Marketing is the process of promoting the products and services offered by the business to persuade the potential customer to take action in favour of the business either through buying the goods or availing the services. Thus, the marketing department is responsible for promoting the goods and services, persuading the customers, and increasing sales. The prime aim of marketing is to make the public aware of the products offered by the business. You will buy a product only when you are aware of its existence, features, and advantages.

Undoubtedly COVID – 19 has affected all the departments involved in the working of a business in different ways, but the hit experienced by the marketing department is the strongest. When you are formulating a marketing strategy, the main aspects to consider are consumer behaviour, consumer preference, and market condition. As you can observe around you, these three variables have been affected severely by the spread of COVID – 19.

5.   HR Department

The human resource department is responsible for ensuring that the business is functioning according to the prescribed guidelines by the state and policies of the business and that the workplace is a safe environment for all employees. This department looks after the personnel aspect of the business. From hiring to ensuring they are comfortable in the workplace, everything comes under the human resource department. The purpose behind the department is the welfare of the employees and the stakeholders. Human resource plays an important role in the smooth functioning of business by solving disputes and maintaining a safe and comfortable environment for everyone. Physical presence in the office helps the HR department to fulfil its duties effectively. Personal interactions are unavoidable for the HR department, and thus COVID – 19 has left a great impact on this department.

6.   IT Department

The information technology department is not traditional, but it is essential for running a business in the digital world. If you own a large business, then you must realize that an IT team is indispensable for functioning in today's world. However, the small business could fill the place of the IT department by hiring a single professional as well. As the name suggests, the IT department deals with the technological aspects of the business. From ensuring a sound Wi-Fi connection in the workplace to setting up a website for the business, everything is managed by the IT department. In a world where everyone is online every time, an IT department makes it easier for your business to cope up with the changing technologies. You must have realized the real value of the IT department after COVID – 19.

Along with these, if a business is dealing with the production of commodities, it may also include manufacturing and purchasing departments. Furthermore, you will often find a customer care department in a large business set-up.

After witnessing the severe effects of COVID – 19, you may like to refer to the working of a business before COVID – 19 as simple. It was COVID – 19 that entangled everything and changed the business world forever. These departments now function differently. COVID – 19 has infected all departments in a business, thus affecting the working of the business.

You

Before COVID – 19 started to infect the world, your life was different. Your morning was different. You woke up every morning with the motivation to work. Even if you are not a morning person, you had to deal with mornings because you needed to work. You sipped your cup of tea or coffee in a hurry to step out of your house. Mornings were clean and clear in the life before COVID – 19.

You knew what you have to do for the day; your life was functioning at a constant rate. Sometimes maybe you didn't even sleep the night before because you were completing the work and used caffeine to keep you awake. Your focus was on working and earning money. Thus, your mornings were sorted and scheduled. Homemade breakfast was not always your option because you were running late for work. You have to beat the traffic and be present before your boss or be present in the meeting to address your employees at the correct time. You would not let breakfast come in your way to work efficiently. But little did you know that breakfast was more important than going fast.

Workplace

When you reached your place of work, it was your daily routine and a warm habit to greet your peers through a handshake or the beloved ones through a hug. Ahh! Those days, when we could see our friends and hug them without any fear of COVID – 19! I am sure your workplace coffee wasn't the best, but you cannot get through your weekday without having a cup of it.

All of us just ignored the simple pleasures of the office. For you, it was your routine, and you continue to follow it without giving much thought because your life was going nicely and who needs a change when everything is fine?

In the computer-driven world also, the importance of printed files and papers was ineffable. Though the presentation will be driven through technology, the notes ought to be ink written for better performance. The technology was undoubtedly an integral part of your work life, but it was only a part before COVID – 19. Personal interactions during office hours helped you to stay motivated and work efficiently. The lunch breaks and chatting with your friends were the best part of your work life. And no feeling could compete with the face-to-face appreciation or celebrating the rise in profit with your team.

Schedule

Your day used to be tightly packed with the work schedule, and you were able to find only a few moments of relaxation, that too rarely. Money and business had become so important in your life that these were the only two things included in your schedule. Weekends were your only excuse to step out of your work life and enjoy yourself, but sometimes the deadline forced you to work during weekends also. Forget about the fun, you had only a little time to take care of yourself and the people around you. The prime concern of your life was to excel at work and earn more to support your lifestyle.

A normal day would start with the worry of work and end with the regret of work not done. In between, you worked and seldom grabbed a bite to survive. Your schedule was designed to survive in the rat race of the world and not in the real world with happiness and health. And your schedule was not changed for a long time as well. Everything was going on smoothly according to the plan: the same routine every hour, every day, every week, and every month. Your diary was filled with meetings and appointments while your doctor wondered why you didn't come to visit him?

Personal Life

The life you have outside your work is known as your personal life. I agree with you when you say that because of the money chasing race going on in the world, you were not able to enjoy your personal life because neither was I. The very concept of me-time was diminishing in the digital world. Whether you are an extrovert, introvert, or ambivert, you will love those few moments only with yourself. The moments when you don't care about anything else and focus only on yourself. You try to enjoy yourself and understand yourself. You play a very important role in your personal life.

Personally, before COVID – 19, I was unable to fit my personal life in my daily schedule. We all were so busy in our meetings and deadlines that we forgot what we owe to ourselves. You dedicated yourself to work, thinking that it will help you to be happy one day. But let me ask you, were you happy? If you gave importance to your personal life, then your answer could be 'yes', but if you completely focused on your work ignoring all other feelings, then you know the right answer and also that it is not the right path.

It was as though it was mentioned in your schedule that your personal life should be ignored. You successfully did this every day. Weekends could be different, but for the majority, your work life dominated your personal life. The main source of your happiness was your family, friends, and relationships. No doubt, these aspects of life can be a little bit complicated, but these only make your life simplified.

I agree that it was difficult to make time to talk to your family daily, but you have to agree that the feeling was priceless. A few moments listening to your mother worry about you and your father giving you life advice was like the energy drink of the day. And how can you forget the fun chat with your siblings and cousins? After all, they are lifesavers. Business and money help you to buy the things that you need to survive, but your loved ones help you to understand the puzzle of life and survive happily.

Before COVID – 19 familiarized the whole world with the concept of quarantine and self-isolation, the weekend's plan with your friends was your way to relax and forget all the worries. Your friends make you realize the importance of living in the moment and enjoying it. Whenever you were down, a warm hug from your loved ones always comforted you and encouraged you to move on. Even if you were hitting a hard point in your carrier, your family and friends were always there to hold your hands and support you.

Celebrating special occasions such as weddings, birthdays and anniversaries gave you the chance to update your wardrobe and dance like no one is watching. Whether it was your work life or your personal life, you have to step out under the open sky to fulfil our roles. You remember all the routes by heart because you travel daily, and you know your routes well because they are part of your routine.

Travel and Transportation

Home to work, work to home, home to party, the party to friend's home, home to restaurants for a meeting, restaurant to work, and then work to home. I guess you are familiar with these routes. These are some general paths followed by all of us in our daily life. Travelling from one place to another is an (old) normal task for us. Travel and transportation were a major part of the daily schedule.

Hours were invested in travelling from your home to work, maybe lots of inconveniences were involved in the route, but it was an important part of your day. You planned your day according to your transportation plans. You invested your time in researching the traffic for a certain day, and then you decided your routes and timings so that you don't suffer delays in your work and in earning money.

You were always travelling from one place to another, meeting new people, and engaging in social interactions for getting through your day while doing your job. You may be a CEO or an employee, but transportation was always included in your schedule. The cheap and quick public transport was the choice of the majority while some preferred personal transport. Some people reasoned that the whole carbon footprint was nowhere near decreasing. The roads used to be filled with the sight of various vehicles and the sound of horns.

Vacation Plans

That one long due vacation is still waiting for you, but in life, after COVID – 19, it might be a little difficult goal to achieve. When we were talking about personal life, then we were definitely including vacations. Everyone has their dream vacations and their plans to travel around the world without any worries. Before you were aware of COVID – 19, you were busy planning a getaway vacation. A vacation where no stress could reach you, and you can explore yourself peacefully.

You would have marked your favourite destination for this vacation. Maybe you didn't save the date, but you were optimistic that soon you would take this vacation and relax. Gaining new experiences by coming out of your hour, maybe the city, maybe country, or maybe the continent was your plan for a vacation. Sitting on the beach amidst the sound of breeze and whisper of the crowd sounds like a nice old plan for a vacation. You were also saving for this vacation. Your budget was set, and your pockets were filling gradually. You were almost ready to set off on the journey of your vacation when COVID – 19 gave you a shock.

Surroundings

Ask yourself the following questions and compare the answers – Where did you spend the major part of your day before COVID – 19? And where do you spend the majority part of your day after COVID – 19? You could easily notice the change in your surroundings. The air might have been polluted earlier, but it was open. You were able to breathe freely without the use of any mask and face shield. Maybe you worked in the office quarters or your separate office, but your social interactions were not restricted.

You were free to choose your surroundings. You could go anywhere and talk to anyone without the fear of COVID – 19.

You could stay in your house if you wished, you could have gone to the mall for a shopping trip or to the nearby café for a delightful cup of coffee. No one restricted your movements, and no pandemic stopped you from enjoying the open sky above and the roads beneath. You met new people on your wish and interacted warmly with people around you. You controlled your schedule and movements, and your decisions were fearless and free.

Desires

To go to the workplace, you needed a mode of transport. Then you needed new apparel to maintain your good look in the workplace and stationery and many other materials used in your business or office work. Your to-do list was a long but monotonous one, and your to-buy list also followed the same pattern.

Your needs did not solely focus on you. Your needs were based on society as well. For example, you could have been happy with just a few pairs of outfits, but for fitting right into the high standard of society, you have to own a lot of them. The different standards of society influenced your needs and desires. You didn't realize that more than the new model of the mobile phone, you needed to upgrade the quality of necessities and focus on your health.

You were living in a free world that was controlled by societal standards. Fear of COVID – 19 was not yet born, but fear of losing your status in society was driving our schedules. Money, business, and other materialistic pleasures were getting the most of your attention while your health, family and friends were waiting for you.

The Story of Jay before COVID – 19

'Jay is a 20-year-old college student. Through observing the functioning of society, he interpreted that earning money is the ultimate goal of life. He decided to dedicate his time and effort to achieve this goal. He scheduled his life concentrating on money. He used to get up early for his college. Then in the afternoon, he went for a part-time job, and in the evening, he spent time hunting for jobs with a better pay-check. His whole life was turned to a strategy to fulfil monetary desires. He didn't care about his health, his relationships, his life, but only about materialism. One day his mom called to check on him, but he didn't pick up because he was too busy with the materialistic chaos. He worked late nights to earn more. He woke up early to attend college and did not hesitate to skip meals to work on this strategy. But in the year 2020, his life changed…' (story follows in unit 2, chapter 1)

LIFE AFTER COVID – 19

Value of Money

Welcome to The Life after COVID – 19, where your perception of money has been changed. Earlier, you might have thought that your life revolves around money, but now COVID – 19 has made you realize that there are numerous things in life to focus on other than money. Your family, friends, partner, and most importantly, your health is eager for your attention. COVID – 19 has reflected the reality and made you realize that money can surely buy certain worldly pleasures, but to experience the true flavours of happiness and comfort, you need to make time for other things as well.

COVID – 19 has acted like a needle that bursts the bubble that labelled earning money as the sole purpose of life. Now everybody, including you and me, is out of that false illusion and can focus on the things that are more important to us. I thought that by devoting time to earning more and more money, I am helping and supporting my family, but after the burst, I realized that my family needs me more than my money. I am sure, like me, you have also realized that money is not the only thing we need to lead a successful and happy life.

Role of Money

It is a very old and wise saying that money cannot buy happiness, but over time, people forgot the deep meaning behind this strong statement. On the one hand, COVID – 19 was frightening the world with its dreadful effects, and on the other hand, it was helping people to realize the real role of numerous things in their life. COVID – 19 made us think about the importance of happiness that cannot be bought with money.

Now in life after COVID – 19, you have realized that money is not the protagonist of your life; rather, it is just playing a supporting role. No one can change the fact that money is the means of exchange in the world market, but how you perceive money in your mind can be changed and has been changed.

We saw in the previous unit that before COVID – 19, the interpretation of money influenced your life decisions such as what job to take; what shifts to work for; to eat or to skip the meal; to visit the doctor or complete the work; to celebrate the festival with family or to stay at the office to earn more and take many more small yet important decisions. But after COVID – 19, we all have taken back the power of money to influence our decisions. By interpreting that earning money is the aim of our life, we were allowing money to exercise control over us. But after COVID – 19, we replaced the role of money with other important aspects of life, such as health and family.

Importance of Money

The designations of numerous things in your life have been changed with the threat of COVID – 19. The fear that no one is safe in this world anymore due to a pandemic attacking our safety has allowed you to revalue money. Profit maximization, income security, more and more earning might be your motto earlier, but now your focus is fitness maximization, family safety, and mental health maintenance.

Now it's easier to understand the true importance of money in our life. You should look at these changes in a positive way. COVID – 19 did not reduce the importance of money in your life; rather, it made you realize that other things that you have been neglecting are worth more - respect, and time. COVID – 19 helped you to re-assign the different aspects of your life the deserving roles according to their true significance.

Survival of the Healthiest

COVID – 19 has brought our attention to one of the most important aspects - health, both physical and mental. The power now lies in the hands of the healthiest and not the wealthiest. The parameters of social status are also transformed. The most expensive diamond is no more the bearer of high status, but the healthiest being is gaining all the praise from the peers. In life after COVID – 19, if you want to make your place in the world then you ought to pay attention to your health. COVID – 19 is a pandemic that is also adversely affecting the world economy.

Skipping meals and completing files late in the night without getting any sleep have proven to be vain. If you still believe that earning money is the purpose of life, then remember that to earn more, you have to stay healthy. COVID – 19 has opened our eyes to the fact that health is wealth. In life after COVID-9, Healthy Hard Work is the key to success. You not only have to take care of your health but also your family, friends, and everyone around you. And you not only have to maintain physical health but also mental health. Exhausting yourself to earn more money is now an obsolete way to work. Taking care of yourself and your peers is the new way to live successfully.

Use of Money

The shift in the value of money has created a change in how we use money. A stroke of realization has hit everybody in this world. You must also have realized a valuable lesson because of the fear of COVID – 19. COVID – 19 is the mirror that allowed us to notice the true reflection and value of various aspects of our life. As we rearrange our list of important things in life, we direct money towards different uses now. Let us understand the post-COVID – 19 use of money by referring to three groups as earlier – low income group, middle income group, and high income group.

Low Income Group

Not much has changed for the low income group, just a few new entries in the group. Due to the economic unrest caused by COVID – 19, you must have noticed people around you losing their jobs or incurring losses in businesses. The majority of us are facing a decline in our income. Thus, the number of people in the low income group is rising.

Similarly, as earlier, the low income group focuses on the necessities. Even the fulfilment of their basic necessities was impacted due to large scale job loss in the unorganized sector. A mass movement from metro cities to their home towns was painfully observed.

Middle Income Group

The myth that money allows you to live happily and highly in society has been busted. The middle income group no longer believes that they need to buy luxuries to impress society. Even if they want to impress society, the new path is through staying healthy and not wealthy. So now, instead of buying the useless showcase goods and services, the middle income group is investing in health products. People have realized that the prime role of money is just to cater to our needs and desires. Now money is directed towards necessities for survival and essentials for maintaining our wellbeing.

High Income Group

You must have noticed that high income groups might be at the top of the list for chasing money, but they were certainly not the toppers when it came to health. They were so busy procuring money that they forgot about their health. But after COVID – 19, their ways have been changed. The high-income group has also chosen a different part and is now concerned more about health care than luxuries. This group is now willing to give up the luxuries that used to make them feel powerful in society and adopt the new normal and focus on the more important aspects that make them powerful in reality. High income groups could afford high quality essentials, and they have started to use their money for this purpose. The group has also realized the importance of the environment and the welfare of society. Since they have access to resources, they have decided to help society as per their capabilities.

In the time of this crisis, environment and society need a hand to help them, and I am proud to say that most of the people have extended their hands for the service. Good deeds are not only associated with the high income group, but also the middle income group. COVID – 19 has made people realize the importance of human life and nature.

You should be proud of yourself if you have also helped society in the time of this global crisis. Remember, never is it too late, and you can help society in many different ways. The biggest contribution to the world during the spread of COVID – 19 is practising self-quarantine and attempting to break the chain of the pandemic.

Some people associated money with possession. We thought that money is ours, we own money, and it should be used for our good. But COVID – 19 made us realize that no one owns the money, and the best use of money is to ensure we survive in this world and help others survive as well.

Money Storage

After the World Health Organisation announced that COVID – 19 is a pandemic, the ways to store money changed forever. COVID – 19 was spreading rapidly throughout the world, and we all were scared and locked up in our houses. You didn't know what could bring the treacherous disease into your house, and thus the thought of using cash also terrified you.

Like you, everyone else started giving up storing cash. Digitization was now helping people to store money easily without the fear of spreading COVID – 19. No one, including you and me, wanted to be a part of the COVID – 19 chain, and thus we started to store money and make payments digitally. COVID – 19 contributed to the decline in the popularity of cash.

Working of Business

With the introduction of digitalization, the business world was constantly changing. The working of business was completely different before COVID – 19.

All sorts of businesses have transformed since the world has witnessed this global crisis. From small scale operations of small business to large scale functioning of large business, everyone is busy planning a new strategy to grow their business. No one ever expected this kind of change in such a short time. Though the primary objective of business remained the same, all short term and long-term goals were changed.

COVID – 19 affected business from various directions. The biggest offshoot was the lockdown. The lockdown was beneficial for your health but detrimental to the health of your business. Lockdown redefined the guidelines to follow and changed the surrounding of the employees. Offices were no more the workplace to carry out your business. Due to the rapid spread of COVID – 19, social distancing was being practised all around you. Both small and large businesses were affected due to these transformations, and they both reacted differently to the situation.

Small Business

Personal interactions and close relationships were the pearls of small businesses. But COVID – 19 has snatched these pearls by injecting the fear of transmission through human contact. Small businesses suffered the most because of the pandemic. During the lockdown, most of the small businesses which do not deal with essential goods and services had to down shutters. This was the case with every technologically backward business.

COVID – 19 marketed the concept of work from home globally. To arrange work-from-home facilities for employees, business had to be technologically advanced and capable. Limited access to resources proved to be a hurdle during the lockdown period. However, the smaller number of employees and small scale of operations were advantages for small business. Since the functioning depended on coordination among a smaller number of people, many managed to save their business. You have to admit that it is not an easy task to manage a small business when all your employees, customers, investors, and the entire public are sitting in their homes without any physical interaction.

You may have noticed that some businesses evolved gracefully and reached new heights, taking advantage of this situation while some businesses had to shut down due to lack of resources. It is your choice and responsibility to uplift your business and help it survive and prosper in life after COVID – 19.

Large Business

Large scale operations imply large scale risks. A large business has more at stake than the small business. Thus, a large business faces the chance of greater losses. COVID – 19 came as a threat to the functioning of many large businesses. To carry out the functioning of a large business, coordination and communication are essential. But due to the ill effects of COVID – 19, it was very difficult to maintain both the Cs. With the lockdown, every business except producers and dealers of 'essentials' had to shut down their offices and hit a pause button on fieldwork.

All employees were delegated work from home responsibilities, and each department was working remotely. It was a challenge for owners of large businesses to arrange effective cloud communication on such a large scale at such short notice. As COVID – 19 and the fear of it penetrated more houses, factories and production units were shut down. Now each employee was supposed to own a device through which he/she could effectively connect with a business.

Easy access to resources and technological advancements helped large businesses to survive during the lockdown period. However, the number of employees and the complex hierarchical structure was an obstruction for smooth functioning.

You might have expected that things would be restored once the lockdown was lifted, but it wasn't the case. Even after the removal of lockdown orders, the business world was entirely changed. Humans fear human contact now. Products and services sold by businesses are being re-evaluated and reconsidered. Consumers are afraid and aware. A large business has a very rigid set of policies, targets, and guidelines. They have to alter everything quickly to adjust to the changing times.

Similar to the small business, some large businesses managed to thrive, whereas some just gave up and distributed their shares. In the time of crisis, it's always your decision whether you want to fight and win or give up the battle and face the losses.

Let us analyze how each department in a general business structure has changed due to the novel coronavirus.

Departments of Business

7. Administration Department

The function of the administrative department remains the same, but the way of functioning has changed. During the lockdown, the administrative department was not able to closely supervise the functioning because they had to manage the business remotely. The sudden changes in the market led the administrative department to alter the guidelines and the policies. The administrative department plays a prominent role in times of crisis. If your administrative department is quick and wise, then the situation can be handled smoothly; otherwise, the business will face a huge risk.

COVID – 19 burdened the administrative departments, and they had to take prompt and proper decisions to save the business. They are the topmost authority in the business. Thus the survival relies upon them. Some steps were skipped, and some policies were reconsidered while facing the consequences of COVID – 19. Small businesses were able to take quick decisions due to the simple hierarchical structure while large businesses were tangled in previous policies. COVID – 19 has declared a race; the business which recovers faster will prosper while the businesses left behind will suffer.

8. Finance Department

Changes in policies, alterations in sales, and shift in incomes affect the finance department directly. With the pandemic hitting the market strongly, the finance department was panicking and brooding over the survival of the business. In addition to that, now the finance department has to manage the accounting remotely. In the digital world, we may say that contacting each other is simple, but for the finance department, it was really difficult to update the data in time while sitting at home.

COVID – 19 has increased the complications for the finance department. With chaos reigning in the world economy, the finance department has to function patiently and smoothly. After the lifting of the lockdown too the business world remained hit.

9. Sales Department

If you dealt with essential goods and services then your business had leverage during the lockdown period. But other businesses were suffering gravely due to the reduction in sales. The needs of consumers shifted with the introduction of COVID – 19 and change in perception of money. If the demand for your product decreases then you will be left with surplus supply which will lead to a reduction in price, ergo reduction in revenue.

The sales department experienced a severe hit due to the pandemic. They were astonished by the adverse effects of COVID – 19. They never witnessed such a sudden and severe reduction in sales of the business product. People were inclining towards home entertainment and essential products while other businesses were barely breathing. Responsible and effective sales departments changed their strategy to attract the target audience with the help of the marketing department.

10. Marketing Department

The first factor that contributes to a business's success is the goods and services offered and the second item on the list is the marketing of those products. COVID – 19 has affected the marketing strategies gravely. Along with COVID – 19, health awareness was also spreading rapidly and widely. People, including you and me, were changing their preferences and choices. They started questioning their previous decisions and made changes in their buying behaviour. Thus, the marketing department was left with a lot of burden on its shoulders.

The department had to make sure to come up with new marketing strategies, arrange campaigns, set new agendas, and change the course of marketing within a short time. It was a very critical time for all businesses. Competition was intense and a slight delay could hold you back from being the customer's first choice. Many businesses introduced new products to adjust to the new needs of the public which led to more work for the marketing department. Even if your business deals with essential products you have to change the marketing scheme to attract the target customers with the new approach involving COVID – 19.

11.   Human Resource Department

As a result of the lockdown, everyone was sent home and assigned work from home duties, but what about the HR department? One of the many aims of the HR department is to ensure that the workplace is a safe and friendly environment for each employee. So, what to do when everyone is in their homes enjoying their comfortable surroundings? The lockdown period was difficult for the HR department. However, large businesses managed to continue the smooth function of this department by optimizing available technology.

COVID – 19 has increased the workload of the human resource department. The department, which earlier maintained a mentally comfortable environment, now has to ensure physically safe surroundings. After the lifting of the lockdown, everyone was confused and scared. You didn't know how to react to the situation. It was necessary to maintain social distancing but how to maintain this distance in offices?

With the help of the administrative department, the HR department has to lay down new rules and regulations and ensure that everyone in the office follows the safety guidelines for COVID – 19 precautions. The cafeteria cannot be the place for office friends to hang out, you cannot allow employees to come in close contact with the customers or other stakeholders.

Other grave decisions taken by the HR department were those related to furlough and laying off. Cost cutting to survive has been a post-COVID reality. Most businesses had to fire at least some employees.

12. Information Technology Department

The most praised department during the lockdown period was the IT department. Due to the need for social distancing, the employees were not able to contact one another personally so technology helped the business to carry out functions digitally. The prime job of the IT department was to create a virtual workspace for all employees and departments. The IT department was certainly the business department during the immediate post-COVID – 19 period.

COVID – 19 also made some businesses realize their capabilities and access to technology in the digital world. The IT department learned that they are capable of managing the business remotely as well. The small businesses were also interested in establishing an IT department after witnessing the dreadful effects of COVID – 19. It was not an easy task to arrange for the whole business to function virtually but you must agree that few businesses performed excellently.

Most companies created infrastructure to enable their employees to work from home. The IT departments worked very efficiently during this. I strongly believe that the processes evolved during this time will benefit the community even after the return of normalcy.

Though each department plays its role and was affected by the pandemic in variegated ways, as a whole the responsibility for smooth functioning lies in the hands of the owner only. Some people feel comfortable to refer their business as their child. Where you have to take good care of it, nurture it, and help it grow. If you manage a business, then it's your responsibility to ensure its safety during times of such crisis.

Some may wonder how Covid – 19, being a pandemic, could affect the working of businesses. The answer to this question is lengthy yet simple. With the rapid spread of COVID – 19 and the increasing number of deaths worldwide, the public was frightened. They didn't know anymore which product is safe for them and which could threaten their well-being. To worsen the situation for businesses, lockdown was imposed in numerous countries. Due to this, people understood the need for necessities and began to focus on healthcare products.

The preferences, needs, and behaviour of customers changed. Small businesses were suffering due to the sudden shutting down, and large businesses found it difficult to manage operations on this scale during the lockdown virtually. The majority of the business is consumer-centric, and due to changes faced by consumers, the businesses were also facing numerous threats.

However, the effect of COVID – 19 on different businesses was based on the industry in which they were functioning. For example, the textile industry witnessed a setback while the online streaming industry celebrated the rise in profits. COVID – 19 has changed the customers, markets, and businesses.

You

Now you wake up in the morning with the motivation to stay at home. Every morning you convince yourself to limit your outings to only necessary work. COVID – 19 is a pandemic, and the more you go out the more danger you call upon yourself. While the motto 'stranger danger' still keeps the kids safe, the new motto 'crowd danger' helps you to protect yourself and people with whom you come in contact. The cup of tea or coffee is now peaceful but confused. You have to work but the methods have changed.

You cannot define your morning as stressful, yet you cannot refer to it as a calm one. **Right after COVID – 19 started to** spread rapidly throughout the world, all the countries started to impose lockdown for the safety of their citizens. Schools, offices, public transport, all were shut down due to this lockdown. People were becoming aware and were practising self-isolation and so were you. Every morning you don't have to hurry for work, maybe you have to attend an online conference, but that does not mean you have to skip your breakfast. You wake up in your bed knowing that all day you have to stay inside the comfort of your house, feeling a bit relieved but worried about the deadlines that you have to meet online.

Workplace

It was easy to differentiate between your workplace and home before COVID – 19 but after the global crisis started to scare the world, your home only transformed into your workplace.

It was like your workplace was absent, so your home came to fulfil the duties as a substitute. When the lockdown forced you to stay within the four walls of your house then you have to go for work from home. From the company CEO to every subordinate employee everyone was using technology as a means to connect to their offices and complete their jobs.

The new workplace was the cloud where everyone could connect digitally and send files in softcopies. You surely miss your office coffee, don't you? From just a part of your work, now technology has become your whole workplace. You use technology for meetings, conferences, and group discussions to ensure social distancing. During the lockdown, you learned that all your office can be confined within the screen of your devices, whether a smartphone or a laptop.

Congratulations! If you are back at your office and you are working under the current situation with precautions. But tell me the truth - is everything the same as before? Does the office staff have the same spirit as before? Do the friendly chit chat moments continue in the office? Are you all still close?

COVID – 19 has not only affected the world as a whole but has also changed your work life. No one in the office is willing to shake hands, not without sanitizer. The smells of sanitizer and the sight of thermal scanning are all over your place of work. You miss that warm hug with your friends without any doubt of infection. A sneeze or cough was always a bad sign but now it scares you to the core. Now, whenever you use the lift the only thought you have in mind is - 'I wonder who used it before me? I hope they were safe and healthy'. The workplace is not as productive as earlier. The stress of the disease, the fear of the spread, and the situation of the world hold you back from doing your best. COVID – 19 brought work from offices to homes and then back from home to the strange ambience offices where everyone is distant and plastic shields are your protector.

If you are still working from home, then you need to rebuild your workplace. Select an isolated corner in your house and redecorate replicating your workplace. Remember too much comfort is an obstruction in the way of productivity. You don't want to sleep during managing your business, do you?

If you are back at office and working in the gloomy workplace under new norms, then try to find small chunks of happiness and motivation in the new normal. The key is to take precautions. If you wear a mask and use sanitizer after using the lift, then you are safe and you could focus on your work. If you avoid touching your face, then you can probably use the office photocopy machine without any fear. Try to take precaution and stay positive.

Priorities

Now you regret all the missed meals? Well, it isn't too late. On witnessing the dreadful situation of the world, you have realized the importance of a healthy body and a healthy mind. 'Strong immunity' is the term jumping around from house to house across the globe. COVID – 19 is a pandemic and it attacks your body, weakens it, and puts all your hard earned money to nought. The fear of COVID – 19 has spread awareness on health. Now you focus on your health better than before. You eat, drink, and consume carefully. Your health has become a priority. Meeting the deadline is important but completing your sleep cycle is your priority. Your body always needed proper attention but you have realized it only now.

Now you don't forget to include healthy food in your schedule and also a session for mental health is listed there. Your post-COVID – 19 schedule respects the fact that health is wealth. Money is secondary, and health is primary. You could use the money to maintain a healthy body but you should not exploit your healthy body to maintain your finances. Your schedule has been shifted from work-oriented to health-oriented. You are taking all possible precautions to ensure that you break the chain of COVID – 19, instead of being a part of it.

Schedule

You should be the priority of your schedule. Your routine should respect your happiness and satisfaction. Work is important but you will be productive only when you are happy. If you want to make a full effort and work efficiently then you ought to work on yourself. The fear of COVID – 19, the lockdown, and the trend of quarantine have made you realize the importance of self-love and self-work. It took you a global crisis to embrace and enhance your personal life.

The sudden deaths caused due to COVID – 19 were a case of utter misery as well as a story of inspiration. You started to understand the value of life and how you should cherish every moment and each and every person. All participants in your life are important, including yourself. COVID – 19 made you understand the real value of yourself and your loved ones. But unfortunately, when you were craving the hug from them, they could not comfort you. COVID – 19 has changed the functioning of social interactions. During the lockdown, when your eyes were slowly opening to the reality of love and warmth, you were lacking those warm moments of love.

However, COVID – 19 taught you to take out time from your busy schedule to pay attention to your loved ones. Your mother does not have to wait for a week to talk to you because you call her daily. Now your personal life dominates your work life on your schedule. No amount of work could keep you away from taking care of yourself and your loved ones. Now you engage in exercises both for physical health and mental health wellbeing.

Now you take care that your body is strong and don't take extra strain, just to earn some extra coins. Your health, family, friends, peers, and your environment are your prime concerns. Money will help you survive but a beautiful personal life will help you stay alive. You decide your schedule and no force such as money could control you. You are well aware of your priorities and no amount of money could influence your choices now. Your health, your family health, your friend's health, and the health of people around you all are important for ensuring a healthy environment.

Travel and Transportation

It seems like COVID – 19 has caused some diversions and now your new route is from the bedroom to the kitchen. If not at present, it had been for a long time after COVID – 19 and during the lockdown. Just imagine how many hours you saved while working from home. No traffic noise, no long routes, no pollution filled roads, just you and your comfortable home. COVID – 19 made the world realize that it not always compulsory to travel and transport. In the digital world, you can finish your work while sitting at home. Work from home was the diversion in your route to work. For the lockdown period, you didn't have to travel to the workplace and thus you can use the saved time productively.

COVID – 19 changed travel and transportation. Even when you have to step outside your home for essential shopping you find that the crowd has disappeared. People are now becoming aware of the fact that social distancing is the key to prevent oneself from the claws of COVID – 19. The roads are not so busy now and the streets are not so crowded. Like you, everyone is stepping out only for necessities. Now you don't look at travel and transportation as an opportunity to visit some place new or with the excitement to travel, but you glance upon it with the fear of COVID – 19.

Vacation Plans

COVID – 19 has hit your optimism hard when it came to your vacation. With the changing world and in life after COVID – 19 enjoying a vacation appears to be a difficult task. Travelling is no longer a fun opportunity; rather, it is a journey filled with fear. The rapid spread of COVID – 19 throughout the world has bestowed on all forms of transportation a bad image. You are no longer comfortable sitting beside a stranger in an aeroplane or sharing your rail cabinet with someone else. The effects of a pandemic have transformed customer behaviour for travel and tourism. Would you call a trip a vacation if it involves you being worried about COVID – 19 throughout the trip? Vacation is all about relaxation and now the best place to relax is within the safe walls of your home.

Surroundings

Just after COVID – 19 when the lockdown was imposed, your powers to decide your surroundings were taken away. You could not just walk outside under the open sky and meet new people. You have to take various precautions and ensure that you spend most of the day inside your house. The fear of COVID – 19 influenced your decisions and your surroundings. Soon the comforts of home were no longer appearing as comfortable to you. You wanted to change your surroundings, go for a morning walk or an evening tea but unfortunately, COVID – 19 did not allow you to do so. You may have disliked your office surroundings before, though now you missed them badly. But you have to stay at home.

Now everything has changed and your preferences also should change. You cannot go anywhere just for fun, neglecting the threat of COVID – 19. You have to be careful and only go to places that are of utmost importance. You are very careful now and you arrange your meetings only in safe surroundings. Now the ambience does not play an important role in selection of surroundings, but safety does.

Desires

From luxury to healthcare, from a new mobile phone model to masks and sanitizers, your needs and priorities have changed post-COVID – 19. Now more than new apparel, you are interested in the stock of sanitizer that contains more than 60% alcohol composition. The spread of COVID – 19 made you realize the importance of health and thus your needs have shifted to healthcare than to taking care of your status in society. The need for showcase goods has declined and you are also focusing only on the necessaries. COVID – 19 has also made a dent on your income.

With the decline in possession of money, you need to direct your income towards essentials and your health. Well, being of physical and mental health should be in the list of your top 5 needs. Nothing is more valuable than your life and health and thus your needs should revolve around these variables only. Now you don't need a new pair of shoes just to compete with your neighbour in society, but you need to build your strength to overpower COVID – 19.

The methods might have changed, but your enthusiasm is the same. You still have the spark to take the turn of success. In life after COVID – 19, you need to adjust to the changes and go forward with strategies that will allow you to grow and progress.

Jay after COVID – 19

'… As he woke up one morning, he read the term Coronavirus while scrolling through the news feeds. It was not much of a concern for him because he cared less for his health and more for money. But as the severity of Coronavirus led to the introduction of COVID – 19, Jay started to read more and inform himself more.

By glancing at the number of deaths and the dreadful spread of the pandemic, he got scared. The threat and spread of COVID – 19 left Jay startled. He began to re-evaluate everything in his life. When he was forced to stay inside his house, he realized the importance of family and relationships. He started to regret every skipped meal and every missed appointment with the doctor. He was scared of the consequences of his previous actions. All his life, he thought he was on the right track and was doing the right thing, but COVID – 19 proved him wrong. His belief that money is the most important thing in life has been shaken.

He knew that now he has to focus on other aspects of his life as well. Earning money was no longer the sole purpose of his life. He started to care. Care about his family, friends, food, health, routine, and lifestyle. Now he believed in a lifestyle that was valued on the qualitative parameters of health and happiness rather than some quantitative amount of money.

But it was difficult for Jay to deal with the sudden changes. He has never faced something so sudden and significant in his life. This experience was new, and he was not aware of how to experience this. The gloomy situation surrounding him made him realize that he misunderstood the value of money his whole life. But now the question was: How to deal with the shift in values?... '

HOW TO SURVIVE AFTER COVID – 19

How to Manage a Healthy Business

Now you have understood the effects of COVID – 19 on the businesses and on your life. Like you, everyone's life has changed, including your stakeholders, and like your business, everyone's business has faced new challenges. This period is extremely crucial for your business. The prime concern during a crisis is the survival of the business, not its development.

COVID – 19 has led to a chaotic situation where you need to use your contingency plans and emergency response strategies. In case you didn't invest your time and effort in such plans then don't panic, you still have time to save your business. The two key points to remember are to take prompt and proper steps. If you follow the correct path ingeniously then the survival of your business stands a greater chance.

COVID – 19 may have shaken numerous aspects of your business, but the foundation is still safe and secure in your responsible hands. You have to establish various pillars to support your business and you have to build new boundaries to protect it. This responsibility can be a bit time consuming but if there will be no business, then where will you invest your time at all?

You can do this. You can save your business. Hold your business with strength and intelligence during this time and crisis.

And then proudly invest in the development of your business. Go and glance at the primary objective of your business. Let the first brick of your business foundation motivate you to help manage a healthy business while a pandemic is infecting the whole world.

The pandemic may have put your business on a ventilator but you can help it breathe again. The whole world has been affected by COVID – 19. Even the industries that are experiencing a significant boost in demand are worried about the limited quantity of supplies available. In simple language, no one could benefit from a pandemic such as COVID – 19. One way or another, everyone is suffering and your period for suffering is over now. You have spent enough time and energy moaning over the losses, now is the time to take action and rebuild your business even stronger than before.

Manage Your Business in Life After COVID – 19

1. Prepare a COVID – 19 Effect Report

The first step towards supporting your business is to calculate the damage caused by the pandemic. You can recover from an injury only when you are aware of its intensity. The proper medication requires proper information. So before formulating any strategies or taking any action first record the losses you incurred due to the spread of COVID – 19.

You can effectively calculate the destruction by comparing the financial statements of your business before and after COVID – 19. Remember, finance is not the only aspect you want to focus on. COVID – 19 has attacked the majority of elements of your business, and you need to analyze the effects of COVID – 19 on these elements. If any department is left unaffected, then you should record that point as well. It will save your time while formulating strategies as you don't have to focus on that department.

If you ignore any effect of COVID – 19 then it can adversely affect the strength of the pillars you are building. For example, if you omit the impact of COVID – 19 on the health of your employees, thinking that it does not affect your business monetarily, then you will have to pay a large cost. If your current employees are not in the best condition to execute new strategies and you did not include the hiring of new employees in your plan then all your efforts will be in vain and your business will incur huge losses.

Surely you have time to recover from these injuries, but you don't have a lot of time. Your success is based on how quickly and efficiently you can take decisions and save your business. You cannot afford to omit a prominent piece of information in the first step itself. You have to look through the intricate details of your business and find the answers. How COVID – 19 has affected all aspects of your business.

Prepare a proper report demonstrating the losses, changes, injuries, and void created by the pandemic in your business. You can use different matrices to prepare this report. From simpler matrices like sales to advanced matrices like return on investment, you can use anyone to produce a helpful report. Only while preparing the report you will realize the importance of this step. As you study the impact of COVID – 19 on your business, innovative and productive healing ideas will start popping up in your mind. Don't forget to note them down immediately.

These will later help you while formulating the strategies and establishing new guidelines.

2. Conduct SWOT Analysis

SWOT is an abbreviation of strengths, weaknesses, opportunities, and threats. SWOT analysis is a simple and effective method to analyze your position in any given situation. During a period of crisis such as COVID – 19, it is essential to perform a SWOT analysis of your business so that you are aware of your strengths, weaknesses, opportunities, and threats.

Strengths and weaknesses are the two internal factors that affect your business internally. Opportunities and threats affect your business externally. You find opportunities and threats in the external environment, unlike the strengths and weaknesses that are found inside your business.

Change is a constant member of the business environment. Even before you witnessed the damage caused by COVID – 19, you have observed the business environment and change. SWOT analysis is an exemplary method to cope with the changes. After recording the effects due to the change in your business, you can focus on the SWOT analysis.

An intriguing fact about the SWOT analysis is the specific sequence in which the elements are arranged. SWOT analysis has a hidden call of action in it. SWOT-analysis helps you to appreciate the strengths of your business, work on the weaknesses of your business, grab the available opportunities available, and neutralize the threats posed to your business. You can also follow these steps backwards that is in the order TOWS.

Strengths: In layman's language, strengths are the functions that your business is good at. You have to consider the elements that stood strong even after the COVID – 19 outbreak to identify your strengths. For example, your social media marketing campaign continues to enjoy success and a significant amount of conversions even after COVID – 19. You have to find out what are the aspects of your business that are supplying power in the time of crisis. So that you can support them to retain the strengths of your business.

Weaknesses: What are the internal elements that pull your business downwards? Find the answer to this question and you will find the weaknesses. After COVID – 19 it has become essential to eliminate the weaknesses. COVID – 19 is causing grave damage to your business, you don't want any internal factor to weaken your business. If you want to manage a healthy business then you have to find out the internal disease. For example, if your business is unable to arrange efficient digital communication for the employees then it can lead to ineffective communication, low productivity, and even low morale in the employees. Thus, you can recognize the application of technology for communication as a weakness for your business.

Once you have identified all the weaknesses in your business you can focus on improving those aspects to transform the weaknesses into your business's strengths. This transformation is generally easy but it requires devotion and concentration. You have to work on your weaknesses to transform them continuously. In the present scenario, you cannot afford to transform all the weaknesses, so instead, you could eliminate them.

Opportunities: When you keep an alert eye on the business environment, you find numerous opportunities that could benefit your business. You might be thinking about what possible opportunities you could have during a global crisis? Well, you haven't tried to find one. There are legions of opportunities around you even at the time of a dreadful pandemic spread. There is always a silver lining in the clouds.

If you find a new opportunity then you get an advantage to grab it early and derive benefit from it. For example, the fear of COVID – 19 has brought numerous millennials back to their home towns and families chilling at their homes. You can use this opportunity and design a campaign to target the reunion of families so that people look at your products from a new perspective and take necessary action in favour of your business. Another example could be the increased use of social networking sites. You could derive your budget from traditional marketing and invest in digital marketing to reach a wider audience.

See, you found the silver lining. It does not matter which industry your business belongs to; you will always find some opportunities to grow and prosper. All you have to do is keep looking and make a clear note to include those opportunities in your future strategies and plans.

Threats: Threats mean the factors present in your business environment that could harm your business. You have already prepared the damage report and you are aware of the losses. But now you have to figure out the external causes of those losses. You might not need an example of the threats posed by COVID – 19 to your business.

Most of the threats posed by COVID – 19 are evident but there are few hidden threats as well. For example, the change in consumer behaviour can be noticed by anyone. Still, you will be able to recognize the adverse effect on the supply chain only when you analyze the business environment.

Once you have recorded the threats, it's time to neutralize them. Your responsibility is to minimize the risks predicted as a result of these threats. You have to transform the threats into opportunities the way you transformed weaknesses into strengths. For example, you can study the changes in consumer behaviour and use it to your advantage, formulate the new marketing strategy based on these observations to gain from the situation.

3.   Establish SMART Goals

SMART goals stand for specific, measurable, attainable, relevant, and time-based goals for the business. For helping your business grow in the time of a global crisis setting SMART goals is an exemplary step. You can establish both short-term and long-term SMART goals. To help your business heal, you should set the targets, and then devote your time and efforts to achieving those targets. Remember, while short term goals will help you record the progress within a short period, long-term goals will help your business prosper in the long run. For example, your short-term goal could be returning to previous sales rates, which will help the business shortly. Whereas your long-term goals should be to increase the sales rates which will help your business develop over a long time. You should consider setting both the targets in the form of SMART goals.

You cannot and should not expect your business to start showing improvement overnight. First, you set the goals, agree on a plan, take necessary actions, and then celebrate the achievement by setting another goal for the success of your business. You ought not to omit any step in between or the consequences will not be in favor of your business.

Now you know the reason to establish short-term and long-term SMART goals, so let's find out how to set them?

Specific: One can achieve a goal only when he/she understands the goal. The goal should be described in a precise and clear manner. The goal should be specific. You should not mention a general topic. You have to encourage your team to work for a specific goal that will benefit your business. The business goals should not be polysemic; rather, they should portray only a single meaning. It ought to be more like a specific command that provides a clear picture of the course of actions to be taken to follow that command or to achieve that goal.

Measurable: You only ask yourself how you will know that you have achieved a goal if it is not measurable. And if you will be unaware of the achievement, then what is the purpose of such a goal? Now you would understand why the goals need to be measurable. You are attempting to recover from a large-scale crisis, and you set a random goal that cannot be measured. Next, you spend your limited time achieving that goal without even knowing if you have achieved it or not? Yes, you have only limited time. No one is going to wait for you, and your stakeholders will move past you if you don't take prompt action and set a measurable goal. Measurable goals ensure that your actions are relevant and utilized instead of being meaningless and going in vain.

Attainable: I want to strengthen my business in life after COVID – 19, and my goal is to increase my sales by 150% within a week. How does this sound to you? Do you want to set such a goal and then end up wasting your precious time and effort? I am sure the answer is 'no'. Unattainable goals not only bring disappointment and pulls down the morale of your business team, but also waste priceless resources. Set an attainable goal so that your team is motivated and your resources produce meaningful results.

Relevant: Business goals should be related to the situation and your business. If you are in the travel and tourism industry, then you cannot set the goals to manufacture better quality products; instead, you should set a goal to improve your marketing reach.

And if **your prime focus** is recovering from the damage caused by COVID – 19, then your goal should not be to search for new stakeholders; instead, the business should attempt to retain old ones. In this crucial period, it is next to impossible to find new investors, customers, and employees (considering the budget that goes into hiring and training) who will trust your business. The business goals should always be relevant so it can benefit the business for the correct cause.

Time-Based: Imagine you just inform your employee to submit an important file and do not specify the deadline. You might wait your whole life to get that file. This is not how business goals should work. To establish useful goals, you should always mention the time limit.

Your team should be aware of the time restriction to produce a quality product quickly. This is a susceptible period for your business, and your business cannot afford to spend any further minutes, try to invest the time in SMART goals, and produce beneficial products for the development of your business.

Example: To reach (specific), the average sales rate (relevant) of 47% (measurable) in 12 months (time-based and attainable).

4. ·Review and Edit Guidelines and Policies

Now, you are aware of the injuries and the different factors that benefit and damage your business. The next step is to establish new guidelines. New guidelines do not imply that you have to eliminate all the previous ones. You have to just amend the old guidelines according to the new normal. While formulating the new guidelines on which your business will function, you have to consider numerous factors such as:

Stakeholders: Stakeholders are the people who impact your business directly and also the people on whom your business has a direct effect such as customers, investors, etc. You cannot amend your guidelines and policies without considering your stakeholders. These are the people who invest their money, time, or effort in your business, and in return they expect you to take decisions in their best interest.

Employees: The new guidelines should address the issues attached to the employee's health and travel plans. The two biggest points highlighted by COVID – 19 is – to take good care of your health and to travel wisely. Since a pandemic is on the loose you cannot let your employees travel the world without any set policies and guidelines. Also, the guidelines should ensure their well-being. For example, social distancing at the workplace is indispensable and masks should be recognized as a uniform for the employees.

Customers: Customers are the destination for the products offered by your business. Customer satisfaction is one of the main objectives of every business in the world. You cannot run a business successfully if your customers are not satisfied with your products and services. Like your marketing strategies, your guidelines should also be customer-centric.

You have to keep the customers safe as well. In small businesses, you come in direct contact with the customers generally. Hence, you have to include strict and polite guidelines for the customers specifying the restriction imposed on social interaction within the workplace. If your business includes delivering your products to the customers' doorsteps, then you need to review the delivery policies — no contact delivery is probably the most popular term in this industry.

Investors: You cannot afford to exclude investors while formulating guidelines and policies. These are the people who provide financial support to your business. They hold the power to bring your business on its knees. The new guidelines and policies should consider the interest of the investors.

Communication Process: Earlier, the communication channels were different. Personal interaction was used for the major part of business communications, but now the compulsion of social distancing has changed it all. You have to consider the communication process while setting new guidelines. For productive results, every business requires effective communication and for effective communication, every business requires efficient channels. After COVID – 19, you should consider shifting the channels to digital platforms.

Online conferences, meetings, and seminars will help to communicate in a time of crisis. When technology allows you to connect with the whole world while sitting on a sofa in your home, you should take advantage of it. You can still seal the deal with your international clients. All you have to do is establish clear guidelines regarding business communication.

Information Releases: These are the crucial times when your business's credibility is at stake. One false information realized by your business and the public starts to look down upon you. You cannot allow any kind of misleading content to be attached to your business. This is a sensitive time, and in the age of the internet, people trust only the businesses that offer them authentic and accurate information. The guidelines should deal with the issue of information release in depth. Whether it is during advertising or during connecting with your customers, you cannot afford any false information to be released with your business's name on it.

Market Condition: How to decide what to do without knowing what is happening? Can you answer this question? If 'yes', then congratulations! and if 'no', then let's find out how to know what's happening so that you can make informed and intelligent decisions. In simple terms, you can explain market conditions as the activities going in the market where your business is settled.

Knowing the market condition assists you in formulating policies and guidelines for the survival of your business. If you know that the market is not functioning well and the demands are declining, then you can take measures to stand out within the market and attract customers through your unique traits. Remember to review the steps taken by your competitors.

Your business guidelines before COVID – 19 may be perfect for life before COVID – 19, but in life after COVID – 19, you have to change them. It is not an option; this is a compulsion.

5. Communication with Stakeholders:

Remember to communicate your new guidelines and policies with your stakeholders. They should be aware that you are taking the necessary steps that will benefit them as well. Communication with stakeholders is extremely important during this time. Everyone is worried about one or the other. The fear of COVID – 19 has shaken the trust of stakeholders.

You do not want the stakeholders to lose trust in your business during such a sensitive period. If you want your business to thrive, then be in contact with your stakeholders. Inform them about each step you are taking to improve the situation and how they will benefit from that.

6. Consider Changes in the Human Resources Department

While the HR department was working for creating a safe workspace for employees earlier, now they have to work for creating a healthy workspace. The new complaints registered in the HR department will be: Mr. X entered my sanitized space to take a pen without my permission. And the new training sessions to be arranged by the human resource department is: How to maintain social distancing seminars.

It is just the tip of the iceberg. The whole HR department has to evolve to contribute to the development of your business.

Now, the HR department has to conduct the training sessions online. New employees will be hired through digital interviews rather than physical interactions. The HR department has to revisit the guidelines and laws.

Along with your business, the state was also establishing new guidelines to adjust to the new pandemic. So now the HR department has to update their books and ensure that your business teams function according to the new rules only. HR departments have to change the way they work. Mental health was always an aspect of HR management. After the lockdown and numerous cases of mental ill-health, the HR department has to prioritize the mental health of the employees. Besides mental health, physical health is also a new priority. The department should ensure that in no way the office turns into a source for transmission of the pandemic. Everyone should be informed about the new guidelines and measures that the business is taking for their safety.

Various new responsibilities were given to the HR department due to the spread of COVID – 19. In my opinion, the most difficult job delegated to the HR department due to this pandemic was firing the employees to meet the new budget. The ill-effects of this pandemic could pose a threat to the productivity of human resources personnel by affecting their mental and physical health. It is the responsibility of the HR department to ensure the well-being of the employees. Precaution from physical health dangers and cure for mental health threats is the core responsibility of the HR department. It is a new way to ensure the productivity of human resources in the business.

7. Formulate New Marketing Strategies

Your marketing strategies could prove to be the lifesaver of your business. Sales increase your business's revenue while marketing increases your sales. Marketing and sales are directly proportional. The wider reach your marketing has, the greater will be your sales rate. COVID – 19 has changed the face of marketing.

The introduction of social media and networking sites was gradually transforming traditional marketing, while COVID – 19 changed everything overnight. With the announcement of the lockdown, everyone was locked in their houses. Now social media sites were the new billboards for businesses and the internet was the new channel to connect with customers. The spread of the pandemic has instilled the fear in everyone's mind that stepping out of your house is dangerous. It led to a prominent shift in consumer behaviour.

In the beginning, people were afraid of online delivery as well. But with the introduction of zero contact delivery, the profits of online shopping shops started to rise. Now it has become compulsory for all businesses that desire to prosper to have a social media presence. People will buy your product only if they are aware of it and they are interested in it. And in the current situation, you can make your customer aware and interested only by approaching them digitally. Traditional marketing strategies will not work in the presence of COVID – 19. No one will dare to open your mail pamphlet; rather, people will search your product on the internet.

For formulating an effective marketing strategy to grow your business during these difficult times you need to follow simple yet smart steps.

Identify your target audience: First, you have to select the group of people you want to rely on for helping your business to survive. You define your target audience using various demographic and psychographic factors. Your whole marketing strategy will be focused on this target audience only. So that when they view your advertisement or your campaign, they feel connected to your business.

Choose the correct platform: As mentioned earlier, now you have to change the channels for marketing. You have to adopt novel digital platforms. The choice of the platform relies on the target audience, business goal, available resources, and budget restrictions. Remember, if you market your product well, but use the wrong platform, you won't receive a response from the viewers. Your content will be created for the target audience, so select a platform where you can attract the target group.

Choose a relevant plan for your campaign: Now COVID – 19 has brought a new concept into light. You can use the trending concepts of social distancing, sanitizing, and mental health to promote your products. Your campaign should be relevant to your product and the current situation. Consumers no longer consume monotonous content. They require new content corresponding to the changing trends. So, include novel agendas in your marketing strategy for recovery.

Connect with the audience: Be sure to include connecting with the audience as a reference point in your strategy. If you want consumers to trust your business then you have to make them feel connected and wanted. The competition is intense and if you need to stand out then you have to create your unique identity in the mind of every consumer that is interested in your product.

Implement the new strategy: Don't expect to get a sudden reaction from your target customers. Once you have implemented your new strategy, keep patience and keep working on innovative ideas to attract more and more people to buy your products and services. Use various features on the internet to ensure they can easily approach you.

8.   Prepare a Proper Budget

Undoubtedly, COVID – 19 had a severe effect on the financial condition of your business. To recover, you need to assign the budget ingeniously. You have to cut down on the extra or unnecessary expenses and incorporate new essentials such as sanitizing the workplace. Along with the new guidelines, you have to prepare a new budget appropriate for the current situation. You can take the help of your old notes to prepare the novel budget.

The purpose of a business budget is to plan the expenditure for the coming financial years based on the financial records of the previous years. A pre-determined structure of expenses restricts the splurging of revenue on irrelevant elements and increasing the savings, ergo increasing the income of the business. In the times of crisis, you should focus on reviewing the budget for the concerned financial year and prepare a recovery budget to allocate the resources for healing your business.

For now, you could consider reducing the workforce and concentrate more on familiarising your business with new technologies to grab the opportunities in the digital age.

Spending more on your IT department will be an excellent decision for your new budget. This budget will help you manage the expenses while achieving your SMART goals set through conducting the SWOT analysis.

9. Fulfil Corporate Social Responsibility

Along with COVID – 19, awareness was also spreading across the globe. With free time at home and access to abundant information on the internet, the public is more aware than ever. Today, your stakeholders are not only interested in the quality of products and returns on investment but are also concerned about your role in the community. Corporate social responsibility is the responsibility that every business owes to society. Society is the source of resources which a business uses to produce goods and services to sell in society and gain profits. Thus, every business should respect and contribute to the betterment of the society in which they function. The ill-effects of COVID – 19 have aroused the immediate need to retain the existing stakeholders and, if possible, you could attempt to attract new stakeholders as well. To do so, you need to establish a noble position in society. Which means this is the right time to fulfil your CSR responsibilities and prove to society that you care about them so that they care about your business in return and save your business from drowning under the effect of COVID – 19.

Now you are fully equipped to pilot your business to new heights. But remember, start with baby steps. First, you have to focus on reviving your business and then growing it. COVID – 19 might have affected your business adversely in the initial stages but now you are prepared to climb the mountain named COVID – 19 and save your business. You can do this. It is not a difficult job to bring back your business on its feet, it may need devotion but it is not difficult for you. You are determined to manage a healthy business in life after COVID – 19. Just follow the tips and you will achieve all your SMART goals while sticking to the budget and implementing the new guidelines, policies, and strategies.

HOW TO MANAGE A HEALTHY MIND?

Physical health has always been a prime focus. You exercise, you keep a check on your diet and you consult fitness experts to stay physically healthy. The old saying also says an apple a day keeps the doctor away. But what about the mental health specialist? Apple won't help you to maintain your mental health. Why is mental health not ranked as important as physical health?

Imagine a bodybuilder who just lost his mother in a treacherous accident and has no friends to talk. He spent his whole life worrying about his physical health and business and now he is devastated. He has a contest the next day, he is well equipped with the strength and adequate state of physical health but he is not mentally healthy. He is distracted, melancholic, and lonely. He loses the contest. Why? Is mental health powerful? Yes. mental health is more powerful than your estimation.

You can put it this way, no matter how strong the body of a car is built, if the engine is inefficient then the car won't work up to its capabilities. Health is an extremely broad term. You cannot confine health to your blood pressure or sugar levels. Healthy means the state of well-being. And well-being is an inclusive concept comprising physical and mental health blended beautifully.

You can be physically fit and yet fail in certain tasks due to your mental inabilities. You have to maintain your mental well-being to succeed. Your emotions control your actions. Your mind controls your body. You cannot allow your mind to be disturbed and your emotions to be tangled. After the spread of COVID – 19, we all believe that health is wealth but one more thing to consider is that physical and mental health together are the keys to success. They are two sides of the same coin, that is, you.

Influence of Mental Health on Your Business

Along with your personal life, mental health also affects your work life. Mental health plays a key role in your business's progress.

1. Concentration

Try to remember the last time you completed a task successfully without concentrating. Anything? No? Well, don't worry, you are not the only one. For finishing a function with fineness, concentration is the essential equipment. With concentration comes intricacy, which helps in producing a high-quality product. But to concentrate you need to keep your mind clear. If you are not mentally healthy then it might be difficult for you to summon the powers of concentration in fulfilling your responsibilities towards your business. Business functions require devotion and undivided attention. You cannot formulate new strategies without concentrating on the issue at hand. A disturbed mind filled with entangled thoughts leads to poor concentration, ergo poor-quality work.

2. Productivity

You are physically healthy and ready to do something productive, but wait! You are not satisfied and something is troubling you. You want to focus on your business and contribute to its progress, but the negative thoughts are not leaving your mind. It is a sign of weak mental health which affects your productivity adversely. Business development demands a productive approach and productivity demands mental well-being. Productivity is essentially required during times of crisis like COVID – 19. If you and your team are productive you can achieve your goals quickly and efficiently. But if you lack productivity, then the consequences will be unfavourable. Mental well-being allows you to process your thoughts and ideas vividly, hence giving a clear pathway to productivity. You will observe that productivity plays a key role in fulfilling your day-to-day responsibilities. From pitching your ideas to clients to finalizing the innovative marketing strategy, everything requires a productive approach.

3. Promptness

How can you take a prompt and proper decision when there is a traffic jam of thoughts in your mind? A clear mind is like the road during the early morning when you can reach your destination quickly without any delay. The rapid spread of COVID – 19 instructs businesses to take prompt action. The more this pandemic is spreading, the less the time available for businesses to rise and shine. One of the prime points in crisis management is promptness. You cannot afford anything to cause delays when it comes to your business. And to keep up the speed, you need to maintain your mental health. A healthy mind means zero hurdles for productive thoughts while contributing to the progress of your business.

Weak mental health tends to infect your promptness and alertness. Anything in your environment could be a disguised opportunity. If you lack alertness then the opportunity will slip off your hand and land in your competitor's palm. If you want to be the early opportunity hunter then stay mentally healthy.

4. Motivation

Motivation is the initial spark that allows you to shine like the sun. Motivation is essential for business development. If the owner is not motivated in the first place, he/she would never launch a business. Motivation is required to start, structure, develop, and prosper. Even a kindergarten student needs the motivation to complete his/her homework, so think about the large businesses' CEOs. Every one of us requires a stick of motivation that will guide us through our path towards success.

Motivation isn't something you possess or earn. Motivation is around you. You can be inspired and motivated by anything in your surroundings. All you have to do is stay alert and keep looking for your motivation. And remember to look for motivation with a **healthy mind. Your emotions interfere with** your abilities to perceive things. You can miss motivation standing right in front of you if you are not mentally fit.

Anxiety and confusion are common traits in such situations. Still, the real businessman is one who overcomes these shortcomings, maintains his mental well-being, and helps his/her business to progress. You cannot deprive your business of motivation. As long as you and your team stay mentally healthy and motivated, no one can come in your way to glory and gain.

5. Decision Making

Emotions, feelings, thoughts, ideas, memories, all of these are packed inside your mind. If you don't handle all these parts of your mind then you will end up in a turmoil. Mental health affects even the tiniest decision in our life. When you are making a decision, you tend to consider legions of factors, including the consequences of your decision.

You may not observe this every single time but your emotions and your mental health influence your decisions. If you are not mentally healthy you tend to take an inappropriate decision. Lack of concentration, promptness, productivity, and motivation would lead you to take a wrong decision that would hurt your business severely.

Decision making is undoubtedly an extremely sensitive and powerful responsibility. You should be able to make the right decision for your business. Otherwise the chances for losses are boundless. It is very unlikely that a disturbed or depressed mind would take a beneficial decision for the business. Promoting mental health implies promoting proper decision making, ergo the progress of your business.

Think, whether a heartbroken entrepreneur who has no one to share his feelings with, will take the correct decision regarding the upcoming major merger?

Influence of COVID – 19 on Your Mental Health

1. Lockdown

The biggest step taken by almost all countries in the world was imposing a nationwide lockdown. The continuous spread of COVID – 19 and fear ensured that all businesses except those dealing with essentials were functioning remotely. From educational institutions to your neighbouring shop, everyone was now online. It is an overwhelming as well as melancholic experience to witness almost the whole world in lockdown. Everyone was sitting in their homes. Everything suddenly changed and your mental health was at stake.

Though earlier you did not pay much attention to your mental health, with caring people around, you felt comfortable. You did not face trouble in the domain of mental health since the world was functioning fine and you had people to share your feelings. Whenever you felt low you could go out for a stroll and walk off your worries.

The open sky had no limits earlier. But after COVID – 19 started to infect the world, you found yourself behind the locked doors of your house. No human contact, no outings, no stress relieving walks, and a great amount of disturbing information intake did not prove to be a great experience for you. You started to feel suffocated in the comforts of your home. You desired to step out but you were restricted. Now there was a limit on access to the open sky. You could not just enjoy the open sky unless it was your terrace or you had to go out to perform some essential job. These deprivations affected your mental health adversely. The existence of technology did not help either.

2. Lack of Human Contact

The new normal introduced by COVID – 19 lacks human contact and warmth of the loved ones. A deep conversation and a hug from the right person could heal your mind. But social distancing forbids you to access this medication. Business activities shifted from offices to homes. Now, you cannot complain to the IT department for your slow internet connection because you are responsible for your workspace.

The little breaks during office time used to be your stress busters. The burden on your shoulders suddenly felt light when you spent a few happy moments with your colleagues. With COVID – 19, the burden of stress increased, but the stress busters were gone. It was no longer safe to enjoy the warmth of human contact. Now social distancing was attacking your mental health.

3. Fear

Every morning, waking up to news of more and more COVID – 19 cases is not the ideal way to start your day. But you had no choice. As the pandemic was spreading across the globe, its fear was entering each household. And fear is not a treat for your mental health. Along with its best friend anxiety, fear was building a permanent house in your mind. It felt like the world was collapsing due to a terrifying pandemic. The peace of mind was lost.

The dreadful effects of COVID – 19 haunted your soul and left you alone with your frightening thoughts. Everyone was affected due to these circumstances. Fear was not a luxury but a necessity during these times. We all were terrified and we all needed to take care of our mental health to eliminate this fear and focus on our and our business's well-being.

4. Sorrow

Blues is not distinctively a sign of ill mental health but not sharing your melancholic feelings could end up harming your health. Regular information intake and reports about people losing their lives and businesses all over the world brought tears to my eyes as well. The ill-effects of COVID – 19, from respiratory issues to economic obstacles, left you startled and sad. The condition around you was not merry. And this sadness affected you deeply.

COVID – 19 as such only affects your physical health. But as you dive deep, you will notice its grave effects on your mental health. And the unfortunate part is that your mental health will be affected whether you are a COVID – 19 patient or not.

5. Large Scale Changes

Most of us are not comfortable with changes. We like the way life goes on. Changes can be introduced but in a long span of time so that we can adapt to them slowly. But COVID – 19 did not consider your feelings. It just changed the whole world within a short period. You did not get enough time to process the changes and the world was already talking about the new normal. So much in so little time left you befuddled.

Confusion about what happened? What to do and what is to come took over your mind. Your thoughts were no longer clear. Everything was tied in an untidy knot which seemed impossible to solve under the given circumstances. You have never experienced such a shift in your entire life and thus it directly affected your mental well-being.

6. Information Intake

It is healthy to be informed, but your mental health gets involved when the question is 'how much to be informed When COVID – 19 was spreading, insensitive and false information was also travelling. The Internet allows you to access abundant information present on the web. With the introduction of social media platforms, anyone could create and disseminate information. There are hardly any filters available in the world of internet.

You were puzzled by the army of information approaching you. Which information is true? Which information is fake? Which information affects me? And which information requires attention? All these questions were dancing in your mind. The flood of information created confusion, disturbance and adversely affected your mental health.

7. Surroundings

From spending most of the day in your office to spending the whole day in your home, the circumstances changed. And this change was not a pleasant one. Initially, you might have felt that work from home was not the worst option to manage your business. As days passed, the effects of COVID – 19 on your business started to grow and your likeness for remote-business functioning started to decline. There is a reason why we are supposed to go to our workplace every day to fulfil our duties. And the reason is the appropriate surroundings. The environment of the workplace motivates you and instructs you to work hard to achieve the goals while the ambience of your home asks you to take a break or rest. Too much comfort is not too good for your business.

You are not accustomed to working from your home. And during this crisis, you need to contribute 100% to protect your business. The inability to work properly within the walls of your home is increasing the burden on your mind. The stress, tension and worries are threatening your mental well-being.

8. Technology Consumption

It was nothing new for you to use technology for business purposes. What's new was using technology to connect with your business team; arranging a virtual meeting with clients; bringing your marketing strategies to digital platforms, excessive hours spent with technology. Mental health specialists do not prescribe technology.

Technology could affect our perception and emotions. Advancement of technology is developing new methods of communication, but nothing is more effective than interpersonal communication. The fear is that even after the spread of COVID – 19 takes a break, the technological shift will not revert. The long hours spent in front of digital screens is going to be the image of our future. You need to prepare your mind to handle the technological pressure on your mental health.

9. Changing Habits

Earlier you woke up, got ready for work, left your home, worked hard in the office to take your business to new heights. You enjoyed your break during office hours, came back home, rested and maybe you went out to taste the flavours of the evening, then slept comfortably in your bed to repeat the cycle the next weekday. What a peaceful schedule. I wish I never had to change my schedule. But COVID – 19 did not consider our wishes. Our simple habits also changed due to COVID – 19. And our mind does not appreciate all these sudden changes.

Now you have to wash your hands for 20 seconds with soap and water and repeat it 20 times a day. You cannot step out of your house without wearing a high-quality mask to protect you from the pandemic. You have to stay at least 6 feet away from any other human being and you have to stay inside your house unless you have some essential outdoor responsibility to fulfil.

How do you think these new habits will affect your mental health? The surroundings changed, work methods changed and now you have to change your habits. As mentioned earlier, it's too much change in too little time. The change in your lifestyle brought about by the dreadful pandemic COVID – 19 has adversely affected your mental health. Your mind wasn't prepared for this battle. You cannot revoke the effects of COVID – 19 on your mental health but you can surely improve and promote mental well-being.

Tips to Stay Healthy

1. Take a Break

Press the pause button. I know you think that you cannot leave your business unattended during this global crisis. But just take a moment and ask yourself: Are you doing it right? Is working long hours helping you support your business or it is just worsening your health? Your business is important and it will get the attention it requires but only after you take a peaceful break to relax your mind.

Breaks are the mantra to maintain mental health and even physical health. Non-stop labour can gravely affect your health. Don't think of these breaks as hindrances in the way of your business's success, but think of it as your recharging period. In the long run, these breaks will help you to make a better decision and develop your business efficiently. Remember that your mind needs a break every now and then. Whenever you feel tired don't hesitate to take a break. It is a contribution to the greater good of your business and mental health.

2. Smile

I agree that COVID – 19 has given you legions of reasons to frown. But to promote mental well-being, you have to find a reason to smile. The more negativity revolves around your mind the more your mental health is affected. The situation is difficult for all of us. We all are together in this. Do not over-analyse the situation and find more reasons to stay low. It is time to be grateful. From blood family to business team you should be grateful for all. Take a moment and cherish your achievements. You can fight against this pandemic and all you need is positivity.

Learn to find happiness in trivial things. The situation might appear as a threat but you have to transform it into an opportunity and take full advantage. Appreciate yourself, appreciate your loved ones. Acknowledge the contributions of everyone and reach out to people to find a reason to smile. Learn the mantra - Positivity drives productivity and stays positive.

3.   Set Attainable Goals

The worst way to treat your mental well-being is by setting unachievable goals. Unattainable goals are destined to end with disappointment and have an ill effect on your mental health. To nurture your mental health, you need to set attainable goals. For example, if your prime focus is your business then attempt to connect with your current customers to retain them. If, just after the chaos caused by COVID 19, you set a target to attract and connect with 10,000 new customers then it will only increase the burden on your health and would result in losing your old customers as well.

Your mind is already going through a lot. COVID – 19 has provided a humungous amount of information to process. Do not increase the weight by setting unattainable goals. When your goals are attainable, you get a chance to appreciate yourself and be motivated to achieve the next target efficiently. Sound mental health requires the music of appreciation and feeling of achievement.

4. Don't Burden Yourself

Assign yourself only an adequate amount of responsibility. Do not attempt to work extra hours to complete extra workload. Stay away from EXTRA. The excessive burden does not suit your mental health nicely. The more burden you carry the less impressive your results will be. Try to complete the tasks one by one. Start with the easy ones and once you gain confidence, then complete the difficult tasks one by one. This way you will finish every task with a clear mind, eliminating the devils of anxiety, frustration and confusion.

5. Share, Share and Share

When you share knowledge, it multiplies and when you share sorrows it divides. It's simple maths applied in mental health. When you share your emotions with other people who understand you, the negative feelings start to fade away. You can't avoid the gloomy feeling, but it is possible to share and let it fade. Sharing your feelings is the best way to deal with them. Some suggest that if you do not feel comfortable sharing your feelings with others, then share them with yourself. Pick up a diary and fill the pages with the ink of your thoughts.

If you are stressed and confused about the future of your business then approach someone you are comfortable with and share your emotions. Tell them how you feel and ask them for advice. In today's world of awareness, numerous professionals are waiting for you to share your problems so they can solve it and earn their living. Do not hesitate to share your feelings with loved ones or professionals. They will always help you and support your mental well-being.

6. Celebrate Small Victories

Don't wait to win the war, celebrate every battle's victory. Don't feel that you do not deserve a celebration. Cherish and celebrate every victory in life. From completing your to-do list to achieving your business targets, you should celebrate all your achievements. Let your body feel happiness and triumph. Let your mind enjoy joy after completing the tiresome task.

7. Focus on Your Goals

You feel puzzled when your thoughts are scattered like the pieces of a jigsaw puzzle. In order to free your mind of unnecessary confusion and turmoil, you need to set your focus. When a dancer performs pirouettes, she fixes her focus on a single point and then starts spinning while focusing her glance on that point. This allows her to perform flawlessly since her focus is fixed. Similarly, when you are attempting to achieve a goal, you should keep your focus determined and avoid getting distracted. It will allow your mind to process quickly and efficiently.

8. Exercise

Whether it is physical or mental you need to exercise to maintain your well-being. Exercise helps you to develop better skills and strengthen your body and mind. You will find numerous convenient mental health exercises. You can practice music as an exercise, you can either play it on an instrument or just relax while listening to your favourite tunes. Solving puzzles is an exemplary mental health exercise for practising alertness and shrewdness. You can also engage in meditation and yoga for calming your mind and feeling the peace. Mental health exercises do not ask for much but offer you very much. With only a couple of hours daily, you can promote mental well-being and productively work for your business.

Employee Mental Health

Along with managing your healthy mind, you need to take care of your employees' mental health. All the employees in your business are an asset and you cannot afford COVID – 19 affecting their mental health and making them a liability. This period is crucial for your life, your business and your employees' lives as well. Like you, their mental health was also attacked with the fear and confusion about COVID – 19. Your business requires the employees to stay prompt, productive, focused and motivated.

Employees' Well-Being

1. Training Sessions

The first step should be to inform all your employees that you are aware of their vulnerability and you want to help and support them. All employees should be educated and trained in the field of mental health. They should be aware of its importance and implications. Most of the time, the person suffering from weak mental health is unaware of the concept itself. So, it is advisable to conduct training and seminars to inform them to educate them and equip them.

2. Counselling Opportunities

Provide them with a channel to share their feelings and problems. Let an expert give them solutions and polish their productivity. Some might consider participating in counselling as unnecessary. But if you offer them free confidential counselling and instruct them to try it once then they will understand its importance. You never outsource a prominent business task to an amateur; that is why you need to consult professionals to help your employees. Approach the experts to make appointments for virtual meetings and ask your employees to share, share and share.

4. Grapevine Communication

Business is like a giant vehicle that needs numerous wheels to function. Informal communication is one of the front wheels. Grapevine communication allows employees to connect and enjoy their office hours. Informal communication is vital for mental well-being. Due to the changes brought by COVID – 19, many businesses are shifting online and employing remote- functioning technology. This eliminates the opportunities for grapevine communication within a workspace.

Even if the employees are coming to the office, they are maintaining social distance and avoiding informal communication. It will certainly affect their mental health and your business adversely. You should ensure that the grapevine channels are still alive within your business. You don't want your employees to work half-heartedly and produce unimpressive results.

If your employees are still working from home, then arrange a virtual office party. Instruct the HR department to encourage grapevine communication and lessen the burden on them. Allow them to enjoy their work so that they can provide you with favourable results.

4. Appreciation

Like celebrating your small victories, you should appreciate your employees' achievements as well. Constant appreciation helps them stay motivated and work efficiently. Let them know that you value their efforts and they play a key role in your business. Instruct all superiors to appreciate subordinates on their achievements and stay polite even if they commit any mistakes. After all, you are planning all this to promote your employees' mental well-being. You don't want a cold-hearted scolding to affect their work. This time is difficult for all of us, so we need to support one another, understand one another and stay polite and positive.

5. Security

Kill all confusion regarding the business and security of their jobs. Millions of people have lost their jobs due to the impact of COVID – 19 on businesses. It has created fear in the mind of every employee. This is a sensitive time and if they are laid off, it would be extremely difficult to get another job. You need to inform your employees about your plans for the business and their jobs. You need them to provide a sense of security so that they can contribute their full efforts for fulfilling their responsibilities.

COVID – 19 has shaken us all, you, me, your employees, your competitors and almost all the people on this earth. Its effects on physical health are evident and frightening. But its effects on mental health are hidden and terrifying. Your personal growth and business growth both will be obstructed if you allow COVID – 19 to infect your mental health. To develop in a time of crisis, you need to stay determined and mentally strong. This global crisis would try to weaken your mental health, but it is your responsibility to stay strong and achieve your goals without any hindrances.

AN OPTIMIST'S EXPECTATIONS FROM FUTURE

All the shifts in variables and the transformation of working methods came as a shock to you. You were amazed to witness this scale of change. But don't worry, you can manage the change. You can manage the shift eloquently. The world around you might be changing, but you are still the same and you can handle all the shift through your determination and strength.

Value of Money

The shift in the value of money and the perception of money should be celebrated. Now people understand the real role of money in their life. You might have perceived money as the aim of life but now you understand that money is just a part of life. This shift is laudable. The meaningless chase behind money had ended and the value of real wealth - health - is now appreciated. You should cherish this change.

It is the right time to go with the flow. The world is now interpreting the value of money differently and so should you. Try to adapt to these changes and adjust to the new values. Now, when you understand the importance of family, health and relationship, you can invest your valuable time in nurturing these essential elements. Don't hurry into understanding this shift in value. Give yourself adequate time to adjust to the new normal and avoid consequent confusion. Money is still the same, only its perception and notional value have changed. Gradually, you will understand the importance of this change and will happily accept the shift.

Working of Business

Yes, a lot has changed in the working of the business. Tradition has been overtaken by technology. Budget problems are making it difficult to adapt to the changes. But you can still manage the situation efficiently. All you need to do is set your priorities.

If budget is a hindrance in achieving your business goals, then set the first goal as securing sound finance. Once the source of working capital is finalised, then move to achieve the other SMART goals. Working according to a fixed schedule will help you to adjust to the changes in the working of the business quickly. Remember to familiarise yourself and your business team with the complications of technology.

You cannot manage the shift without the application of technology. Every crisis brings together the efforts of the whole team. It is the right time to showcase your teamwork and move towards success even when a pandemic is infecting the world. Remember that you have to transform the threats into opportunities and grab them to your advantage. You have to apply your strengths to rise from this decline and work on your weaknesses to transform them into strengths.

You

More than anything in the world, you have been affected by this pandemic. The change in your habits, decision-making approach and perceptions have left you startled. The confusion is not unusual, but if you manage it patiently then it will be unusual and impressive. A change was always a part of your life, but you never experienced this sudden and large-scale change. So, it may be a slow process, but eventually, you will adapt to the new normal and be accustomed to the new habits such as wearing masks and using sanitizers. Don't let the fear of COVID – 19 affect your mental health. Try to exercise and handle your emotions efficiently. Stay healthy and stay active to manage your personal and work life eloquently and fruitfully.

The Story of Jay

"…Jay was confused and concerned. He didn't know how to react to this shift and adjust to the changes. But he did not allow this confusion to cloud his peace of mind. As the first step, he talked to his family and friends and peacefully analysed the situation. He did not jump into any conclusions until he was fully equipped. Then he decided to lay out his plans for the future. Starting with easy and necessary goals, he gradually shifted to progress and prosper plans. He knew that patience was the key to manage a crisis like COVID – 19. His job was shifted online, and he was familiarizing himself with advanced technology. Earlier, he hesitated to invest time and effort in personal growth, but now he focused on his health and skill development. This shift proved to be the star that led him to the correct path."